contents

The following pages represent my best efforts to understand and articulate how to write software to create a more beautiful world.

Sep Kamvar
January, 2015
Cambridge, Massachusetts

Syntax & Sage

Sep Kamvar

Illustrated by Kim Smith

ISBN 978-0-692-56363-2

Illustrations by Kim Smith.

Farmer&Farmer
PRESS
CAMBRIDGE, MA

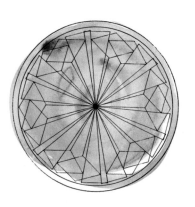

part one: mastery and mimicry

in which I describe some design principles for technologies that follow nature. In short, such technologies would be self-limiting, accessible, mutualistic, and purposeful. My hope is that technologies that follow these principles will lead to a greater unity between art and science, between intuition and reason, between nature and machine. Each would nurture the other.

self-limitation

surf and silicon

I moved to Palo Alto in 1999, at the height of the dot-com boom. I was at Stanford, which felt like the epicenter of it all. Every week I would hear about a hot startup or new technology trend. It was an exciting and frenetic time.

On the weekends, I would go surfing in Santa Cruz, about an hour south of Palo Alto, where the pace was different. One day, I was talking about all of this to a man who had been surfing at Pleasure Point for 40 years.

You have everything you need right here, he told me. Look at it. Good surf, good friends, this sunset. The problem with having a lot of stuff, he said, is that at some point the stuff starts ruling you.

mastery

A recurring theme in science fiction is the idea that one day, our technologies will become self-aware, grow their population, and take over the world. Of course, humans will still be around, otherwise there's no story, but they will be second-class citizens to the tools they invented.

I've often wondered why self-awareness always comes first. Perhaps it's because it makes for a more interesting storyline. After all, a technology doesn't need to be self-aware to be self-reinforcing.

A few years ago, Nielsen ran a study that showed that the average teenager sends more than 100 text messages a day. Adults might get startled or nostalgic when they hear this, but the kids, for the most part, are all right.

They like being in touch with their friends, and are not so concerned about the fragmentation of their attention or their dependence on their devices. Their phones are an extension of themselves.

If there were a textbook example of a viral technology, SMS may be it. Its use facilitates its spread. People get texts, and they respond. The responders then at some point become initiators, and the story goes on. Eventually, even the kids who don't want to be attached to their phones don't have such an easy choice. In a culture where everybody sends each other 3,000 texts a month, you get left out if you only send 30.

There is a story of Bill Joy asking Danny Hillis what he thought about the scenario in which humans one day merge with robots. Danny responded that the changes would come gradually, and we'd get used to it.

That's the way it is with technology. We get used to it. I will get older and sound like a Luddite when I suggest that a hundred text messages a day might be too much. That will simply be the pace of modern life.

When the mechanical clock was invented, one of its early uses was to set the arrival and departure times of factory workers during the industrial revolution. At the time, people hated the idea of getting to work at a certain time; it felt like the ultimate victory of machine over man. Now, it's seen as responsible behavior.

But if aliens come from outer space and see people wake up grudgingly every morning to the beeping of an alarm clock, they might wonder who is the master and who is the tool.

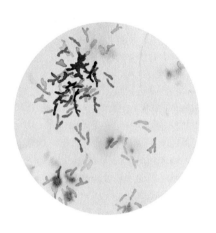

natural limits

Inside of each of us, there are about 10 trillion human cells, and about 100 trillion bacterial cells. By cell count, we are only 10% human.

Given how outnumbered we are, it's surprising that we don't die more often from bacterial disease. You might expect that, of the hundreds of species of bacteria that live inside of us, at least a few would get out of line and start growing at our expense.

We can give credit to antibiotics for saving us, but I think that would miss the point. Even before antibiotics, a surprisingly small number of people died from bacteria, considering how many of them we host. And if we could invent an antibiotic that would get rid of all bacteria, we wouldn't want to. Our bacteria help us digest our food, store our fats, produce our vitamins, and train our immune systems.

The truth is that we are not alive in spite of the hordes of bacteria that inhabit us. We are alive because of them.

To me, one of the most startling and beautiful properties of our bacteria is their intricate ability to keep themselves in check. Let's take, for example, bifidobacteria. This species of bacteria lives in our gut and secretes acetic acid, which in turn breaks down the carbohydrates we eat and protects us from certain infections. Remarkably, and luckily for us, the acetic acid produced by our bifidobacteria also keeps them from growing out of control. When the environment gets too acidic, they don't reproduce.

Perhaps I shouldn't be too surprised by this feat of selflessness. Relationships tend to develop a rich texture as they mature, and we and our symbiotic bacteria have been going at this for some time now. I'm reminded of an older couple, where both partners have their quirks, but each knows how far to go, when to pull back, and what to tolerate; where each knows the other so well, and is so dependent on the other, that it's hard to tell where one person stops and the other begins.

The relationship between us and our technologies is newer, like a younger love. It's fiery and exciting, and we're still learning our boundaries.

Technologies, like most things, have natural limits to their utility. Up to a certain point, e-mail makes us more efficient. After that, the mounds of e-mail in our inbox take time away from our real work. Up to a certain point, time spent on social networks brings us closer to our friends. After that, it takes away from time we spend with them in person.

Which brings us back, again, to our bacteria. If we want tools that respect their natural limits, we can design limitation into the tools themselves.

If the idea of self-limiting tools seems antithetical to technology and capitalism, let me suggest that we already build them. A search engine is a self-limiting tool. As is an online dating site. When these tools succeed, people leave the site. Video games and TVs, on the other hand, are self-reinforcing. Their use doesn't lead to disuse; their use leads to more use.

The more self-reinforcing a technology is, the more likely we are to use it at our own expense. On the other hand, the more self-limiting a technology is, the more likely it is to die out.

The key is to find the balance.

accessibility

production by the masses

In 1930, Gandhi spent 8 months in the Yerwada Jail
in Western India. During that time, he invented a new
spinning wheel that came to be known as the Yerwada
charkha. The Yerwada charkha is one of the more
beautiful pieces of technology I've seen; it's elegant, easy-
to-build, and efficient.

Gandhi made the spinning wheel a linchpin of his
independence campaign. And it worked. By spinning their
own cloth, poverty-stricken villagers gave themselves a
source of income and spiritual sustenance. They freed
themselves from their dependence on the British textile
industry. And they spawned an ecosystem of trades, from
weaving to dyeing to washing to carpentry, that restored
vibrancy to the villages.

It has always intrigued me that Gandhi spent so much time thinking about technology. I understand the wisdom of it, but it's rare to see such technology-centric activism. It would be like today's leading civil-rights leaders urging their constituents to learn how to program mobile devices.

So I find it ironic that Gandhi's critics labeled him as anti-technology, although I can understand why they did. Gandhi fiercely opposed expensive technology. And at the time, modern technology was expensive technology. If you opposed the factory, you opposed modernity.

But what Gandhi understood is that tools are most useful to the people that own them.

And villagers didn't own factories.

what lies upstream

We use tools to build our tools. We use an ax and hammer to make a cabin, and we use Python and Apache to build a web service. These upstream tools are crucial in shaping our society. A world with no hammers would have no houses.

Most upstream tools are so ingrained in our culture that we often forget that they are tools at all—like our languages, educational systems, markets, and governments. But it is important to remember that these are tools, and as tools we can shape them, rather than allow them to shape us.

Our tendency as toolmakers is to want upstream tools that are powerful. I'd argue that it's more important to have upstream tools that are accessible.

By all accounts, Oracle is a more powerful database than MySQL. But if only one could exist, I'd prefer MySQL. Because MySQL is free—for use and for modification—it fosters a broader ecosystem of builders. It enables anybody with time and knowledge to build a tool to fix a problem they see in the world. It allows people to build things and regift them to the developer community. We would not want a web that's shaped only by those who can afford Oracle.

When upstream tools are only accessible to a few, our tools are more likely to foster monoculture rather than a vibrant ecosystem, subservience rather than self-determination. This is why Gandhi advocated the spinning wheel over the textile factory. And it's why people don't want WalMart in their community, barriers for startups, or money in politics. In the same way that we don't want a web that's shaped only by those who can afford Oracle, we don't want a world that's shaped only by those who can afford factories, or lawyers, or senators.

The web, for the most part, gets this right. Most web services are built on top of free operating systems, databases, web servers, and programming languages. They are marketed by accessible tools like Facebook and Twitter and Adwords. And they are often funded by accessible funding sources like Y Combinator, or Kickstarter, or by sales through App Stores. The pace of innovation on the web, and the outsized role that software has played in shaping our lives, is in large part because these upstream mechanisms for production, distribution, and financing are more available than they are in other industries.

This suggests a guiding principle for makers: Look for upstream tools that are powerful, and work to make them more accessible. Square and AWS are nice examples of this. So are inexpensive 3D printers.

The corollary to this principle is: Look for upstream tools that are accessible, and make them more powerful. The recent efforts around JavaScript are nice examples here.

Like the sun, our upstream tools should be accessible and empowering to all.

mutualism

the cuckoo and the wildflower

The Great Spotted Cuckoo is a nomadic species of bird that lays its eggs in the nests of the smaller European Magpie. If the magpie host removes the cuckoo's egg from her nest, the cuckoo ransacks the nest and destroys the eggs. When the baby cuckoo hatches, the magpie feeds it along with her own chicks. But the baby cuckoo is bigger, takes more food, and will often kill the magpie chicks by pushing them out of the nest.

Of course, this is dangerous, not just for the magpie, but for the cuckoo itself, who will at some point run out of nests to invade. In contrast, consider the wildflower, that reproduces by providing pollen to bees and butterflies and nectar to hummingbirds. One spreads quickly at the expense of the ecosystem that sustains it. The other spreads slowly, as a side effect of nourishing its ecosystem.

When we build our tools, we should aim for the latter.

software ecologies

If we're ever feeling smug about our position at the top of the animal kingdom, it is humbling to consider that we live in the company of more than a quadrillion ants. For each person on this earth, there are a few hundred thousand ants, bustling about, building cities, having children, waging wars. We might, with some imagination, see a little of ourselves in them.

To me, ants are fascinating for another reason. They challenge our concept of self.

An individual ant is a feckless creature. It wanders around aimlessly, seeming to have no ability or purpose. But when you get a lot of them together, it's like alchemy. They transform into creatures that astound us with their intellect.

I remember reading an article a few years ago about how ant colonies eat. The authors studied 20 colonies of green-headed ants, and described a remarkably elaborate feeding process that can best be described as a collective mouth and gut.

The food for each colony was collected by worker ants, exactly according to the needs of the colony. The workers extracted the carbohydrates, which they could eat, and then fed the remainder to the larvae in the nest, who require high-protein diets. The larvae ate and then fed the remainder back to the workers, who could better digest the processed protein, and anything left was taken out of the nest by the workers and dumped as waste.

The process is so reminiscent of digestion in higher-order animals that it makes you wonder, which is the organism: the ant or the colony?

If I were to try to describe the mechanism for the emergent intelligence in ant colonies, I might use two words: communication and gift. A passage from E. O. Wilson's novel, *Anthill*, describes this nicely:

"The members of the Trailhead Colony transmitted their messages using about a dozen chemical signals, which they picked up by smelling one another constantly with sweeps of their antennae. An ant who was well-fed said to a less well-fed nest mate, 'Smell this, and if you are hungry eat.' If the ant approached and was in fact hungry, she extended her tongue, and the donor ant rewarded her by regurgitating liquid directly into her mouth."

Thinking about ants and their networks of communication and gift, I can't help but think of the internet.

In 2005, the programmer Paul Rademacher reverse-engineered the JavaScript code for Google Maps, wrote a program to scrape Craigslist apartment listings, and overlaid the Craigslist listings on Google Maps. It was the first web mashup.

It's hard now to appreciate how clever that was at the time. Today, mashups are the norm. Most web services offer free APIs, and it's common for people to use multiple APIs to build something more intelligent than any of the individual services. APIs serve as a mechanism for communication and gift.

In retrospect, web services and APIs were a logical extension of blogs and RSS. What one did for text, the other did for software. This is common in the history of technology. New paradigms tend to start in technologies that are cheap to build, and spread to technologies that are expensive to build. They spread from text to software to hardware.

By that token, I imagine we will soon see more hardware APIs. Our phones will communicate with our cars, and our cars will communicate with our home thermostats. People will build hardware controllers that combine multiple APIs to coordinate our devices in surprising and thoughtful ways.

But that is an easy prediction. To see further into the future of hardware, we might look at what's happening with text today. When we look at Twitter and SMS, we still see communication and gift. But more strikingly, we see smallness.

If software follows text, I imagine we'll start to see lots of APIs that do small things. But they will easily interact with one another together to do big things. And if hardware then follows software, I imagine that we will see lots of small devices that do simple things alone, but complex things together.

They might remind us of ants.

missions and metrics

There is an old Zen story about a man riding a horse, galloping frantically down a path. His friend, who is sitting by the side of the road, calls out, "Where are you going?" The man replies: "I don't know. Ask the horse!"

When we build our tools, we depend on metrics to help guide our development. We keep graphs of unique visitors and pageviews and watch them closely. This keeps us honest. It's hard to convince anybody that we're building a useful tool if our metrics show that nobody is using it.

But we must take care when we use metrics. Metrics can be like the horse in the old Zen story. Once we decide on them, they have a habit of setting the agenda. As the old adage goes, what gets measured gets managed.

The standard metric for a country's economic welfare is GDP. I find this strange. If the government decided to print money in order to give gifts to the CEOs of large banks, that would increase GDP. So would clearcutting our national forests to build strip malls, outsourcing the raising of our children, or incarcerating large swaths of our poor.

If we temper the language a bit, change a few words here and there, we might find that this scene is not so far from reality.

My point is that metrics shape behavior. Joseph Stiglitz describes this mechanism nicely: "What we gather our information about, and how we describe success, affects what we strive for." Political leaders who want to grow the economy, he says, will focus policies on things that increase GDP, even when GDP does not correlate with societal well-being.

Which brings me to my second point: All metrics leave something out. Often, they leave the most important things out.

In 2007, Stanford offered a course called CS377W: Creating Engaging Facebook Apps. The course assignment was to build a Facebook application that, according to the course website, would "focus on solving a problem for a broad audience." It was an intensively metrics-driven class, and the key metric was user numbers. By the metrics, the results were astonishing: In the course of the 10-week term, the apps collectively reached 16 million users.

The flip side was that the applications themselves were underwhelming. Most of them allowed users to do things like rank the attractiveness of their friends, send virtual hugs and have virtual pillow fights. The substance of the applications reflected what the metric left out. If it were possible to measure the value of a user's attention, or how enriching an application is to her life, the course projects would likely have been quite different. But sometimes, the important things can't be measured.

It is useful, therefore, to have missions to balance our metrics. Of course, each tool should have its own mission. But if I were to suggest one mission for all tools, it might be this: Every tool should nourish the things upon which it depends.

We see this principle at varying levels in some of our tools today. I call them cyclical tools. The iPhone empowers the developer ecosystem that helps drive its adoption. A bike strengthens the person who pedals it. Open-source software educates its potential contributors. A hallmark of cyclical tools is that they create open loops: The bike strengthens its rider to do things other than just pedal the bike.

Cyclical tools are like trees, whose falling leaves fertilize the soil in which they grow.

At both ends of the stack, all tools depend on

nature and human nature. They depend on the sun, trees, minerals, and fossil fuels to provide their raw materials and energy. They depend on the creativity of builders to give them form. And they depend on the attention of their users, without which they would languish.

An ecosystem of cyclical tools would therefore nourish nature and empower people. A fully cyclical software application may, for example, use peer-to-peer data centers powered by its users, consisting of biodegradable, fertilizing microprocessors. It would be open-source and provide APIs to empower the creativity of builders, and a clean design and useful purpose that cultivates the concentration of its users.

If some of this sounds like science fiction, so did manned lunar vehicles in 1950, or self-driving cars in 2000. We have a tendency to achieve what we focus on.

It's difficult to build cyclical tools because the alternative is so tempting. Cars are faster than bikes. FarmVille reaches more people than *Animal Farm*. At first, cyclical tools appear to be lower-power, slower-growth, and more expensive than extractive tools.

But you can't measure the impact of tools on their own. You must measure them by the ecosystems that they co-create.

purpose

heart and head

The great scientists of Ancient Persia were also artists. Omar Khayyam was an astronomer and a poet, Ibn Sina was a medical scientist and a poet, and Shaykh-i Baha'i was a mathematician and an architect.

Today we see this less. Artists are mostly artists, and scientists are mostly scientists. And generally, our technologies derive from science. Since science aligns with the head, and art aligns with the heart, understanding the heart and the head helps us to understand our modern technologies.

Our heads cultivate reason. Our hearts cultivate intuition.

Our heads seek opportunity. Our hearts seek purpose.

Our heads maximize utility. Our hearts give gifts.

Our heads think of self. Our hearts feel connection.

Today, our technologies reflect reason and utility and opportunity and self. But this may be an artifact of our time. We could equally imagine building technologies that reflect intuition and purpose and gift and connection. I might say we're already starting.

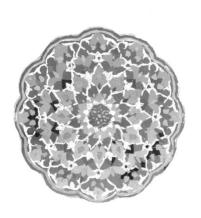

the nature of computer programming

The twig girdler is a species of beetle that lives in Texas and Northeast Mexico. When the female is ready to lay her eggs, she finds a mimosa tree, crawls onto a branch, chews a slit into it, and lays her eggs. But her larvae can't survive in live wood, so then she backs down towards the trunk, chews a groove around the branch, and the branch falls off. She then flies away and a few weeks later, her eggs are hatched and her larvae feed on the dead wood of the branch. What's most amazing is this: a mimosa tree, unpruned, will live for about 25 years. A mimosa tree, pruned by twig girdlers, can live for over 100 years.

How this complex, beautiful relationship came to be is one of the mysteries of evolutionary biology. The odds of getting to it just from random mutation and natural selection are slim.

But we don't need to understand the mechanism to characterize the effect. The effect is as if the beetle has some intuitive sense of the world around her, as if the beetle and the mimosa tree are connected, as if they both exist with the unique purpose of helping one another by offering life-affirming gifts.

We see this again and again in nature. It is as if nature acts out of the properties of the heart.

It's OK that we don't yet understand the mechanism. I'm reminded of something that Feynman said about quantum physics: "I think I can safely say that nobody understands quantum mechanics. So do not take this lecture too seriously, but just relax and enjoy it. I am going to tell you what nature behaves like. If you will simply admit that maybe she does behave like this, you will find her a delightful, entrancing thing. Do not keep saying to yourself, if you can possibly avoid it, 'But how can it be like that?' Because you will get down the drain, into a blind alley from which nobody has escaped. Nobody knows how it can be like that."

I make this point because I want to draw a distinction between biomimicry—which examines the mechanisms of nature and attempts to replicate its apparatus in technology—and the kind of technology that I'm proposing. The most powerful qualities of nature are those where we don't yet understand the apparatus.

We don't fully understand nature's wisdom, her purpose, her intuition, her connection. But we can mimic these qualities without understanding their mechanisms, because they parallel the qualities of the heart.

If we want to build technologies that follow nature, we will motivate them from the heart. Of course, we will use our heads to make them work. But our choice of the tools we build—and the attitude with which we build them— will come from a place of gift and purpose and intuition and connection. In this respect, we will be artists as well as scientists.

I think the best programmers understand this. Don Knuth, who wrote the book on programming, pointedly called it *The Art of Computer Programming.*

In his 1974 Turing Award lecture, he said: "My feeling is that when we prepare a program, it can be like composing poetry or music. Furthermore, when we read other people's programs, we can recognize some of them as genuine works of art. I can still remember the great thrill it was for me to read the listing of Stan Poley's SOAP II assembly program in 1958; you probably think I'm crazy, but at the time it meant a great deal to me to see how elegant a system program could be. The possibility of writing beautiful programs, even in assembly language, is what got me hooked on programming in the first place."

And Bill Joy, who built vi and BSD (both of which

are still used some 30 years later), once wrote about how Michelangelo released statues from the stone, carving as if he were discovering the form rather than creating it.

"In my most ecstatic moments," said Joy, "the software in the computer emerged in the same way … I felt that it was already there in the machine, waiting to be released. Staying up all night seemed a small price to pay to free it— to give the ideas concrete form."

gift economies

When people talk of gift economies, often they talk about them as a replacement for the market economy. But gift economies and market economies have operated side-by-side for much of history. Child care, until recently, was exclusively a gift economy—neighbors would babysit one another's kids. The creative arts and science have historically been gift economies, and to a large extent they still are. And today, free, open-source software sits alongside ad-supported and paid software.

To me, the most interesting examples of gift economies are when they exist alongside money economies within the same organization. I think this points to where the world is headed. Craigslist doesn't charge for any

the heart of the builder

Over the past few years, there has been a meaningful trend in the design community towards user-centered design. As with any methodology, it's valuable to a point. User-centered design is great for designing a new toaster. But it's not so useful in designing, say, the World Wide Web. If you asked people in 1989 what they needed to make their life better, it was unlikely that they would have said a decentralized network of information nodes that are linked using hypertext.

The danger in user-centered design is that it releases the designer of the responsibility for having a vision for the world. Why have one when we can just ask users what they want? But this is a very limiting mindset. The user sees the world as it is. Our job as builders is to create the world as it could be.

It's not that users are less intelligent than builders. They just tend to underestimate the possibilities of a technology, and therefore suggest incremental changes. Other than Mark Zuckerberg, there were few people in 2004 who saw that Facebook could become an identity system for the web. Instead, most of its users had ideas on customizing the profile page, or sending event invitations, or whether or not to allow high school students to use the site.

There is another reason to avoid relying on your users to design your tool. The most elegantly crafted tools are those where the purpose of the tool aligns with the purpose of its builder. So the key to building great technologies is to first find your purpose. And you will not find it by polling your users.

Instead, you might be better served to spend time in places where you can see reflections of yourself. The best surfers I know seem to have a sense of exactly where the next wave will be. They craft a style about their surfing and their life that seems to come directly from the water. Artists that I admire seem to be quiet and quiet and quiet, and then come up with something beautiful, as if the beauty came from some relationship with the silence. And the great programmers I know are always taking breaks from the screen to go walk in the woods, as if they receive the most difficult parts of their programs by osmosis, and then just go to their desk to type it up.

Organic technologies arise from the heart of the builder, from a place of gift, from an intuition and purpose outside of oneself. There is something beautiful about the fact that spending time in nature helps get us there.

part two: make space for beauty

in which I explore how software shapes our environment,
which then shapes ourselves. I discuss the foundational
importance of human attention and its relationship to
compassion, and I suggest some ways that software can
foster physical environments to nourish attention. It is
useful, in envisioning such environments, to focus on
how they make us feel. It is useful, in other words, to pay
special attention to beauty.

flow

I was talking, the other day, to an acupuncturist friend of mine, and I asked him how he heals people. He told me that he doesn't heal people. He introduces small interventions that unblock the flow of energy in the body, allowing the body to heal itself.

In software, we think about user flows rather than energy flows. We know that if we make something easier to do, more people will do it. This alone sounds obvious, but it's surprising how sensitive this relationship is. Small changes in design can create big changes in behavior. I remember, when I was working at Google, we would make a button just a little bit more visible, and millions more people would click on it. It felt like magic.

Or perhaps I should say that it felt like acupuncture.

sensors for life

In the vineyards in Northern California, the vintners plant roses at the end of each row of vines. The roses are beautiful, of course, but that's not why they plant them. They plant them because Northern California is home to a fungus called powdery mildew. This fungus kills grapes, but it kills roses first. Blooming roses, then, are a signal that the environment will sustain grapes. They are sensors for life.

Once you see the roses in the vineyards, it's hard not to see them everywhere.

In the year before I left San Francisco, food trucks started sprouting up all over the city. It was a curious phenomenon and I started asking around about it. This food truck renaissance, as it turns out, was powered by Twitter.

It was difficult, at the time, to get a food truck licensed in San Francisco. But with Twitter, unlicensed food trucks could thrive. They would park in a different spot each day and tweet out where they were.

The legal food trucks, at a certain point, caught wind of this. They started following the followers of the illegal food trucks, who, in turn, followed them back, and a community was born. This community worked to change the regulations, and when they did, even more food trucks came onto the streets.

In other words, software was shaping the city.

Food trucks are cheap and easy, relative to most changes in the city. We should expect them to appear first. But their presence indicates something deeper. It indicates an environment that can sustain informal networks of small, independent producers.

This all suggests a new way to engage in urban design. If we have a vision for the city, we might start by creating something small—a single public microgarden, a single shopfront school, a single parking-lot plaza. We can then design a social process that helps other people create their own version of that thing. And finally, we can write software to make that social process easier. In this way, we will see lots of small things start blooming in our cities.

The food trucks are the roses in the vineyards.

soft fascination

I have been thinking, of late, about the Mayan temples.

These temples, along with the aqueducts and reservoirs of the Mayan golden age, are wonderful feats of technology. They are a testament to the human capacity to make great things. They are also, equally, a testament to the availability of trees. To heat one square meter of the limestone plaster used to make these temples, the Mayans needed to burn 20 trees.

Today we live in a golden age of software. On the backs of our software frameworks we have created a highly connected and communicative global society. I may now, without thinking much of it, access the biggest encyclopedia in history from my bedroom, and hail a private car with a supercomputer that lives in my pocket.

As the Mayan temples were fueled by trees, our software is fueled by another natural resource: attention. Through software, we have remarkable reach into our collective attention. A single website can reach billions of people; a mobile app can notify me when I'm in my car. Attention is a powerful force, and collective attention is one of the most powerful forces we have. We may harness this force to create great things.

But we must take care. The flip side of being able to easily access the attention of others, of course, is that others can easily access ours.

There is a beautiful short story by Kurt Vonnegut, called "Harrison Bergeron," in which intelligent people are required to wear an earpiece that is always interrupting them with a distracting sound, not allowing them to complete any thought that takes more than a few minutes to formulate.

I am reminded of this story each time my phone buzzes.

The psychologists, of course, have looked into this, well before my devices started giving me pause. The fragmentation of our attention, they tell us, leads to a decline in thoughtfulness, in deliberation, and, most prominently, in compassion. We are less kind when we are distracted.

Perhaps this is why we have seen a rise, in recent

years, of things like meditation and Montessori. They are conservation practices for our attention. Meditation reserves a time of day (like the early morning) to cultivate concentration. Montessori reserves a time of life (early childhood) to do the same; Maria Montessori referred to the development of concentration as "the most important single result of our whole work."

These practices are not so different, in spirit, than the Mayan practice of cultivating sacred groves of trees that could not be cut down. One reserves time to conserve attention, the other reserves space to conserve trees.

But there is more, here, than metaphor.

I remember reading, a few years back, a wonderful book by the psychologists Rachel and Stephen Kaplan, in which they developed a theory called Attention Restoration Theory. In this book, they introduced the notion of soft fascination. As opposed to hard fascination, which refers to patterns that grab our attention—a billboard in Times Square, an incoming text message, a video game—soft fascination refers to patterns that readily hold the attention, but in a serene way that permits a more reflective mode—a butterfly on a wildflower, the song of a nightingale, the movement of leaves on a tree. Soft fascination, they showed, is a powerful restorative measure for attention.

This suggests a path for us as makers of space. It

suggests a path for makers because, while it's always possible for people to make individual choices, the default choices are most powerful.

It is possible, individually, to create a practice where we take time each day to go into nature, but it would be easier if nature were present on our daily walk to work. It is possible, individually, to limit our children's use of tablets, but it would be easier if our early-childhood environments were peaceful spaces where children could work with beautiful materials that gently hold their attention.

So perhaps the best way to cultivate our collective attention—and with it, our collective compassion—is through the deliberate design of our environments. We can work to shape our environments to foster soft fascination, so we can experience small sacred moments scattered throughout the day. To begin, we don't need grand gestures. Even a single tree on a barren street has a noticeable effect.

If we keep at it, we might find ourselves reshaping the city.

And we might find, in turn, that the city will help to reshape ourselves.

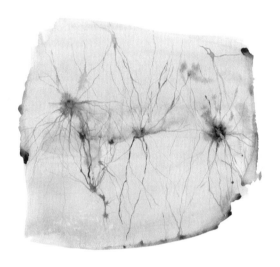

artifice and intelligence

We are constantly surprising ourselves with what we discover in science. We think we have something figured out, and then, suddenly, we see something that changes everything: an electron goes through two slits at the same time, or an acquired trait is inherited. The whole business keeps us on our toes.

We surprise ourselves in the social sciences as well, which is itself surprising. We have, collectively, thousands of years of experience with one another. You'd think we would know ourselves pretty well by now.

But we keep going along, surprising ourselves at each turn.

Take, for example, how we make decisions.

For a long time, the great Western thinkers—from Plato to Descartes—thought that decision-making is, or at least should be, a rational process. The very word decide comes from the Latin root *decidere*, which means to cut off, suggesting a mental process by which a range of options are cut off to settle on a final one. Our emotions, said the great thinkers, have no place in reasonable decision-making.

We thought we had this all figured out when, in 1848, a young man named Phineas Gage sustained a head injury that left him unable to feel emotions. Surprisingly, he also lost his ability to make decisions. We've seen this natural experiment repeated, again and again, in modern patients who have sustained damage to their prefrontal cortex. Losing our capacity to feel makes us unable to decide. Without emotion, reason flails.

I imagine we are just beginning to scratch the surface of this whole decision-making thing, and there are other experiments that give us room for wonder. In one study, humans with serious heart disease expressed less emotion than those with healthy hearts. In another, changing the bacteria in the stomach of a mouse was shown to change its decisions.

We have, as it turns out, brain cells all over our body. Our heart and gut, in particular, are little satellite brains; there are 100 million neurons in our gut alone.

They communicate with a little part of the brain in the front that is responsible for integrating our emotions into our decision-making processes. Our ability to make decisions—and more generally, our intelligence—depends on our emotions, which in turn, depends on our bodies.

Perhaps we shouldn't be so surprised. We are told, when we are making a big decision, to listen to our heart, or to go with our gut feeling.

Nevertheless, I think it will take us some time to fully wrap our heads around this—or should I say wrap our bodies around this. Once we do, I think it will change the way we think about artificial intelligence.

The roots of artificial intelligence are based in the tradition of rational decision-making. If making a decision just involved looking objectively through a space of options and choosing the best one, then our computers could do that quite well. And in fact they do, when we restrict the domain to tasks suited to this sort of intelligence, like playing chess or classifying an image. All we need to do is give the computer an objective function.

But deciding the objective in the first place, that requires a deeper intelligence; one that, for now, seems inseparable from our ability to have emotions. And perhaps this holds a key to what truly makes us human. The computers, they can think—in many cases better than we can—but, for the foreseeable future at least, they will need us to *feel*.

make space for beauty

Students of computer science get taught, at places like Stanford and MIT, how to make things. But they don't get taught—at least not in a traditional computer science curriculum—how to decide what to make. This is because, in the industrial model of work, they would not graduate into a world where they had much of a choice. They would work for a company that would tell them what to make.

But as software has gotten less expensive to make, so, too, has it become more entrepreneurial. We find ourselves responsible not only for building things, but for deciding what to build. And in doing so we face a question that we were not taught to answer in school: How do we decide?

I was thinking about this question the other day when

I heard a story on the radio about birdsong. The guest, an ecologist who studies sound, noted that humans have a bandwidth of super-sensitive hearing between 2.5 and 5 kilohertz. This is surprising, he said, because the normal human voice is much lower—between 500 hertz and 2 kilohertz. So human hearing is not matched to the human voice.

But there is, he said, a perfect match in nature: birdsong. Our hearing evolved to hear even the faintest birdsong. And why? Because birdsong is a primary indicator of habitats prosperous to humans.

This is a fairly recent conversation in the quantitative sciences; it was started less than 100 years ago. But we were able to act for thousands of years without yet knowing the science. Our ancestors followed birdsong to flourishing habitats, because birdsong is beautiful.

So how do we decide what to make? It is tempting to apply our quantitative skills to this question, to analyze the data and decide based on the numbers. There is a place for that, of course, but I wouldn't begin there.

I would begin, instead, by tapping into our well of feelings to see what makes us feel peaceful, feel sublime, feel alive, to see what fills us with wonder and hope. I would begin, in other words, by tapping into what is beautiful.

If we create, inside of ourselves, a respect for beauty,

then we will create beauty outside of ourselves. And in doing so, we might find that beauty is not entirely subjective. We might find that cultivating a keen awareness of our own feelings is not so different from understanding the feelings of others. We might find that what makes us feel peaceful makes others feel peaceful, that what makes us feel sublime makes others feel sublime, that what makes us feel alive makes others feel alive. We might find that what fills us with wonder and hope fills others with wonder and hope. We might find that what is beautiful to us is beautiful to others.

And we might find that in that beauty there are truths that science has not yet discovered.

Make space for beauty.

part three: succession

in which I describe human-scale systems of production
that foster autonomy and individuality. I discuss the role
of the software engineer in catalyzing these systems, as
the designer of frameworks that create environments for
agency. These frameworks begin an ecological succession
towards large-scale gift economies.

watson

We are a remarkably efficient species, although we
never give ourselves enough credit for it. The human
brain uses around 25 watts, about the same amount
of power as a desktop fan or an aquarium heater, and
with that performs about 10 quadrillion calculations per
second, about the same as all the computers in the world
combined.

When you consider this, it puts into perspective some
of our recent achievements in artificial intelligence. It was
a big deal when IBM's Watson supercomputer became the
Jeopardy grand champion, a more difficult task than Deep
Blue beating Kasparov. But Watson uses about the same
amount of power as 30,000 human brains. And it can't
even tie its own shoe.

If we want a more fair fight, we could pit Watson against a team of 30,000 people. We would need to find some way to coordinate that 30,000-person team, of course, and we'd probably need some software to do that. But that software would be a lot simpler than Watson.

Here is a little algorithm that should work: To start, each team member gets 10 coins. Any time Alex Trebek gives a clue, team members may ring the buzzer as long as they have at least one coin. Everybody who rings the buzzer has 4 seconds to answer, and in the last second the software tabulates all the responses and returns the most common one. The team members who get it right get an additional coin. Those who get it wrong get a coin taken away.

There are variants of this algorithm, of course. We can weight each response by the number coins the respondent has. Or we can give more coins for getting the harder clues right.

My point is that, once we consider the true efficiency of a human, we start thinking in a different way. The technology we design has a lighter touch; it aims to aid our natural capacity for intelligence rather than replace it.

And I don't want to limit myself, here, to intelligence.

We see the same story in mobility. A mid-sized car gets a little over half a mile per kilocalorie of energy. A human walking gets 10 miles per kilocalorie. Even if we exclude the cost of the car, the cost of the road, and the cost of the infrastructure we build for fueling, walking is still 20 times as efficient as driving.

There does exist a vehicle that is more efficient than a human walking: a human on a bicycle. A human on a bicycle gets 25 miles per kilocalorie, the equivalent of 750 miles per gallon. Like my fictitious Jeopardy software, the bicycle is a light-touch technology, that extends the human's natural ability for mobility rather than replacing it.

I imagine we may, one day, create vehicles that go 25 miles per kilocalorie, or machines that are able to think and feel and perform a few quadrillion computations per second on 25 watts. I don't discount this possibility.

But in the meantime, I'd like to make a modest proposal: Let us design tools to enhance our fantastically efficient human capacities, and environments to exercise them. Let us make cities that are walkable, roads that are bikeable, jobs that allow us to think, and environments that foster our natural ability to heal.

Even if we ignore the efficiencies, we might find that we'd enjoy it.

environments for agency

Technologies have power not just as tools, but as metaphors.

AirBnB, for example, is both a tool to help you share your home, and a way to describe ideas that, prior to AirBnB, would have been difficult to imagine: an AirBnB for cars, an AirBnB for office space, an AirBnB, even, for dogs.

We tend to underestimate the power of technologies as metaphors, because after a while, we stop using the metaphors explicitly. Modern day fast-food joints, call centers, farms, big companies, and schools all came from the metaphor of the factory, even though people no longer say, as the dean of Stanford's School of Education did in the early 1900s: "Schools should be factories in which raw products, children, are to be shaped and formed into finished products."

The factory metaphor has been especially potent in our culture because of its promise of efficiency, and there is something to that claim. Efficient processes make complex things possible. It is hard to imagine an artisanal process for making a commercial aircraft.

But the efficiency of the factory comes at the expense of ingenuity. The factory worker has the natural capacity for ingenuity, but the assembly line gives him little opportunity to use it. The system requires him to implement other people's ideas: "Weld this piece to that one." Without agency, the worker's ingenuity begins to wither.

If we want to create environments for agency, we would be well-served, instead, to look to small-scale systems of production. Agency is inherent in these systems, since they don't create a distinction between those who have ideas and those who implement them.

The startup is one example of such a system. Startup founders are modern-day artisans, and indeed startups tend to be wellsprings of ingenuity.

There are other examples as well: in education there is the one-room schoolhouse, in transportation there is the small bicycle design shop with a 3D printer, in agriculture there is the small-lot permaculture garden. These systems all offer the people involved more agency than the industrial systems that dominate today. In many ways, they remind me of the past.

But I might predict one difference between the small-scale systems of the past and the small-scale systems of the future. The gardens, the bicycle design shops, the one-room schoolhouses of the future, they will produce at a small scale, they will make decisions at a small scale, but they will talk to one another at a large scale. They will be decentralized, but not disconnected.

When these systems do come, we will be prepared for them, because they will resemble another metaphor, one that I think has more staying power than the factory. If we stand back far enough and squint, we might find that they look like the internet.

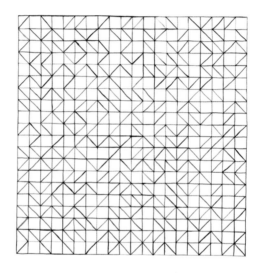

half the story

A few years ago, I read something Toni Morrison wrote about the first sentence in *Song of Solomon*. She detailed how each word was picked carefully in a way that sets up the rest of the story. She wrote two pages about this one sentence, and it was clear that she could have written many more. I remember feeling something I had felt throughout the novel: that it expressed so much meaning in so little space.

I think programmers are particularly sensitive to this sort of beauty. It goes to the heart of what we do. Our programming languages give us the ability to express complex ideas compactly, and this is what allows us to write powerful programs in a reasonable amount of time.

In many cases, it is what allows us to write them at all. It is in its poetry that programming has its power.

But programs are different than poems, at least on the surface, in the way they achieve their density of meaning. Programs are concise and precise, while poems are concise and ambiguous. We can infer several meanings from the same line of poetry, because it is written to let us do so. The poet gives us a framework, to which we can add our own meaning.

Or, as Jay-Z puts it, more concisely, "I tell you half the story, the rest you fill it in."

Some artists take this idea a step further. When you buy a Sol LeWitt piece, you don't buy a completed drawing. Instead you buy a piece of paper that says something like: "Using a black, hard crayon, draw a twenty-inch square. Divide this square into one-inch squares. Within each one-inch square, draw nothing, or draw a diagonal straight line from corner to corner …"

Songs by the musician Cornelius Cardew give instructions to the chorus that look like: "Sing this line of text 3 times, each time for a length of a breath, on a note of your choosing."

In these pieces, the artist, through a series of instructions, both tells a story of what the piece could look like and defines a social process to make that story a reality. The artist builds a framework, and the community fills it in.

And now this starts to look, again, like software.

A program, we must remember, is both a programmer's series of instructions to the computer, and the resulting program's series of instructions to its users. The instructions to the computer are defined by syntax, while the instructions to the users are defined by interfaces.

In well-designed software, the instructions to the user tell a clear story of the world the programmer is trying to achieve, though the best ones maintain some ambiguity. They tell a user to communicate publicly in 140 characters, or to edit an encyclopedia entry, but they don't specify which characters or which entry. The magic happens when a well-told story meets an imaginative set of users.

And so, the art of software becomes the art of coming up with a beautiful story of a world that could exist, and then telling that story in code (half the story anyway) to the right set of users.

I notice that this art, as I've defined it, is broader than the traditional art of programming. It is available to those who have the freedom to choose the software they write, who see their task not only to write code, but to come up with a beautiful story and find the right set of users. It is available, in other words, to the entrepreneur.

To such people there is tremendous power, for programs are more direct than poetry. They act on the world. They give a framework not just for human thought, but for human behavior. The stories that these programmers tell, if they tell them well, are likely to become realities.

It is important, therefore, to be thoughtful, to be wise, to be kind, to tell the stories that, when they become realities, will help to heal society.

This is a difficult job, and not one that entrepreneurs should have to take on alone. In most arts, there have been curators and editors, who have had a point of view, who have defined movements, who have nurtured artists not just based on their likelihood for success, but based on a shared story, a shared vision for the world. Our museums may play this role; but I think, in this realm, it would be a more natural job for our venture capitalists.

They, too, must tell beautiful stories.

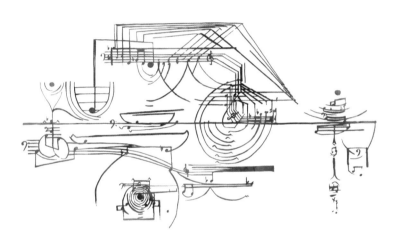

homestead

In 1862, Abraham Lincoln signed into law the
Homestead Act, which gave people 160 acres of free land
simply for agreeing to live and farm on it. It was, from the
perspective of the settlers, a great gift. It allowed them to
do something that they hadn't been able to do prior to the
grant: to become small farmers, to work for themselves. It
gave them agency.

The economist Hernando de Soto has used the
Homestead Act as an example of how much economic
development is possible with the right legal mechanisms
to property, and I imagine this is true. But for me, the
Homestead Act makes me think of something else. I think
about how much agency is possible with the right gift.

in the direction of dreams

There is a lot of money to be made in software platforms. But that doesn't mean they will be expensive to their users. On the contrary, the most valuable platforms tend to gravitate towards being free. In fact, it is because they are valuable to so many people that they have a tendency to become free.

A big platform may start out being expensive. The early movers in a space may choose to charge a large fee, as Microsoft did to its customers, or a big commission, as Uber does to its drivers. They then reinvest that money back into the platform, which makes it difficult for new entrants to compete on product, at least initially.

New entrants can, however, compete on price. If

they are able to establish prices low enough, they can get enough market share to allow them to invest more money into the product. The improved product in turn serves to increase market share, which in turn enables more investment in the product. Eventually the less expensive platform becomes just as good or better than the initial platform, and at that point, it is only a matter of time before it dominates.

It doesn't always play out this way, and in fact it rarely plays out this way when a platform is niche and its users are rich. (Bloomberg, for example, will be expensive for a while.) But it does work this way often enough that many platforms will choose to be free from the beginning.

In many cases, the only sustainable way to be free is to be open-source. Bitcoin can be free in a way that PayPal cannot. And open-source platforms establish, either explicitly or implicitly, open standards that let the platform interoperate with others.

We see this dynamic most clearly in programming tools. Our dominant web servers, databases, programming languages, version control systems, editors—the list goes on—are all free, open-source, and interoperable.

Our programming tools comprise the most mature ecosystem in software. They have been around since the beginning of computers, and they might give us a glimpse into the future of our younger software ecosystems. If so, we should expect that more major platforms will become free, open-source, and interoperable, like our dominant browsers, operating systems, and encyclopedias have recently done.

Some will do so out of a generous spirit of their creators, and others will do so out of the rational calculations of the companies that start them. The sum effect, regardless of the motives, is that we will create the most valuable gift economy in history.

Indeed, we already have.

Fireweed

There is a beautiful species of wildflower called fireweed; it is named so because it is typically the first plant to colonize a field after a forest fire. Fireweed grows well in damaged soil, spreading bursts of color even in areas affected by an oil spill. In World War II, these beautiful flowers covered the craters left by bombs.

Fireweed is a pioneer species—it spreads quickly to cover a damaged landscape and its roots put nitrogen back into the soil, increasing the soil's fertility and beginning a chain of ecological succession that ultimately leads to a healthy ecosystem. Once its job is done, it dies off, but its seeds remain in the ground for many years, ready to blossom once again when needed.

notes

 Mastery

Nielsen. "U.S. Teen Mobile Report Calling Yesterday, Texting Today, Using Apps Tomorrow." Last modified October 13, 2010. http://www.nielsen.com/us/en/insights/news/2010/u-s-teen-mobile-report-calling-yesterday-texting-today-using-apps-tomorrow.html.

Joy, Bill. "Why the Future Doesn't Need Us." Wired, April 2000.

Mumford, Lewis. Technics and Civilization. London: Routledge, 1934.

 Natural Limits

Marchesi, Julian R., ed. The Human Microbiota and Microbiome. Boston: CAB International, 2014.

Bezkorovainy, Anatoly. Biochemistry and Physiology of Bifidobacteria. United States: CRC Press, 1989.

Schumacher, E. F. Small is Beautiful: Economics as if People Mattered. London: Blond and Briggs, 1973.

Production by the Masses

"Gandhi Invents Spinning Wheel." Popular Science Monthly, December 1931.

 Software Ecologies

Dussutour, Audrey and Stephen J. Simpson. "Communal Nutrition in Ants." Current Biology 19;9. (12 May 2009): 740-44.

Wilson, E. O. Anthill. New York: W.W. Norton & Company, Inc., 2010.

Ratliff, Evan. "Google Maps Is Changing the Way We See the World." Wired, July 2007.

 Missions and Metrics

"Joseph Stiglitz: Inequality and Future Prosperity," by William Cohan, asiasociety.org, April 9, 2013, http://asiasociety.org/video/joseph-stiglitz-inequality-and-future-prosperity-complete?page=76.

Heart and Head

Khayyam, Omar. Rubaiyat. Translated by Edward FitzGerald. Boston: Houghton, Osgood and Company, 1878.

Sina, Ibn. The Book of Healing. 11th century, exact dates unknown.

Baha'i, Shaykh. Kashcool. 16th-17th century, exact dates unknown.

The Nature of Computer Programming

Thomas, Lewis. Late Night Thoughts on Listening to Mahler's Ninth Symphony. United States: Penguin Books, 1983.

Feynman, Richard P. "Quantum Mechanics." The Messenger Lectures, Cambridge, MA, 1964.

Knuth, Donald E. "Computer Programming as an Art." Turing Award Lecture, San Francisco, CA, 1974.

Joy, Bill. "Why the Future Doesn't Need Us." Wired, April 2000.

Gift Economies

Eisenstein, Charles. Sacred Economics. Money, Gift, and Society in the Age of Transition. Berkeley: Evolver Editions, 2011.

Sensors for Life

SFGate. "Planting Rose Bushes With Grape Vines." Accessed April 9, 2015. http://homeguides.sfgate.com/planting-rose-bushes-grape-vines-29763.html

Gubler, W. D. and S. T. Koike. "Powdery Mildew on Fruits and Berries." Pest Notes 7494 (January 2011): 1-4.

Anenberg, Elliot and Ed Kung. "Information Technology and Product Variety in the City: The Case of Food Trucks." Proceedings of the annual meeting of the American Economics Society, Boston, Massachusetts, January 3-5, 2015.

Soft Fascination

Turner II, B. L. and Jeremy A. Sabloff. "Classic Period collapse of the Central Maya Lowlands: Insights about human–environment relationships for sustainability." PNAS 109; 35 (28 August 2012): 13908-14.

Vonnegut, Kurt. "Harrison Bergeron." Welcome to the Monkey House. United States: Delacorte Press, 1968.

Kaplan, Rachel and Stephen Kaplan. The Experience of Nature: A Psychological Perspective. England: Cambridge University Press, 1989.

Artifice and Intelligence

Russell, Stuart and Peter Norvig. Artificial Intelligence: A Modern Approach. 3rd ed. United States: Pearson, 2014.

Macmillan, M. "Phineas Gage - Unravelling the Myth." The Psychologist, 2008, 21: 828-831.

Collins, Stephen M, Zain Kassam and Premsyl Bersick. "The adoptive transfer of behavioral phenotype via the intestinal microbiota: experimental evidence and clinical implications." Current Opinion in Microbiology, 16;3, (June 2013): 240–5.

J. A. Kline, D. Neumann, M. A. Haug, D. J. Kammer, and V. A. Krabill. "Decreased facial expression variability in patients with serious cardiopulmonary disease in the emergency care setting." Emergency Medicine Journal, 2015;32:3-8 doi:10.1136/emermed-2014-203602.

 Make Space for Beauty

On Being. "The Last Quiet Places: Silence and the Presence of Everything." Accessed April 9, 2015. http://www.onbeing.org/program/last-quiet-places/4557.

 Watson

Jabr, Ferris. "Does Thinking Really Hard Burn More Calories?" Scientific American, July 18, 2012. Accessed January 10, 2015. http://www.scientificamerican.com/article/ thinking-hard-calories/.

Murphy, Tom. "MPG of a Human." Do the Math, November 29, 2011. Accessed January 10, 2015. http://physics.ucsd.edu/do-the-math/2011/11/mpg-of-a-human/.

Environments for Agency

Cubberley, Ellwood. Public School Administration. Boston: Houghton Mifflin Company, 1922.

 Syntax and Sage

Morrison, Toni. Preface to Song of Solomon. United States: Alfred Knopf, 1977.

Jay-Z. "Dead Presidents II". Reasonable Doubt. Roc-A-Fella and Priority Records, 1996.

LeWitt, Sol. "Directions." Work from Instructions. Canada: Nova Scotia College of Art and Design, 1971.

Cardew, Cornelius. "Treatise." England: Peters Edition, 1967.

 Homestead

Annals of Congress, 37th Cong., 2nd sess., 392.

de Soto, Hernando. The Mystery of Capital. United States: Basic Books, 2000.